Ducks for DARK Times

Michael Leunig is an Australian cartoonist
who tries valiantly to live in Melbourne where
he was born, but often he seeks refuge in the bush
of north-eastern Victoria. *Ducks for Dark Times*
comprises pieces that have previously appeared
in *The Age* and the *Sydney Morning Herald*.

The Penguin Leunig
The Second Leunig
The Bedtime Leunig
A Bag of Roosters
Ramming the Shears
The Travelling Leunig
A Common Prayer.
The Prayer Tree
Common Prayer Collection
Introspective.
A Common Philosophy
Everyday Devils and Angels
A Bunch of Poesy
You and Me.
Short Notes From the Long History of Happiness

Why Dogs Sniff Each Other's Tails.
Goat person
The Curly Pyjama Letters.
The Stick
Poems 1972-2002
Strange Creature
When I Talk to You.
Wild Figments
A New Penguin Leunig
Hot
The Lot.
The Essential Leunig
Holy Fool
Musings from the Inner Duck
The Wayward Leunig

Ducks for DARK Times

MICHAEL LEUNIG

PENGUIN BOOKS

PENGUIN BOOKS

UK | USA | Canada | Ireland | Australia
India | New Zealand | South Africa | China

Penguin Books is part of the Penguin Random House group of companies
whose addresses can be found at global.penguinrandomhouse.com.

First published by Penguin Random House Australia Pty Ltd, 2017

1 3 5 7 9 10 8 6 4 2

Copyright © Michael Leunig 2017

Cover design by Michael Leunig and Adam Laszczuk © Penguin Random House Australia Pty Ltd.
Colour separation by Splitting Image Colour Studio, Clayton, Victoria
Printed and bound in China by Leo Paper Products Ltd.

National Library of Australia
Cataloguing-in-Publication data:

Leunig, Michael, author.
Ducks for dark times/Michael Leunig.
9780143788577 (paperback).
Caricatures and cartoons – Australia.
Art and popular culture – Australia.
Australian wit and humor, Pictorial.

penguin.com.au

A Note From the AUTHOR

Ducks for Dark Times is my twentieth collection of cartoons. As with those previous volumes, the offerings in this one were all produced for newspaper publication, in response to news items and editorial concerns of the day. Many of these pieces, perhaps most of them, may not seem related to worldly issues or events, but in one way or another they were all created after the daily parade of human horrors, wonders and absurdities had been digested – they are a sort of speaking back to fate, to the astonishing universal reality as I understood it at the time.

Sometimes a cartoonist's response to the human condition is one of dismay and protest, sheer despondency in the face of powerful political or cultural systems that just keep repeating their stupid atrocities in the name of goodness and righteousness. Sometimes it is disgust wrapped in a wry moral observation. And often a cartoon is simply an attempted antidote to the growing madness, a flight into whimsy, lyrical humour, and childlike visions of a fairer and lovelier world.

On certain occasions, humorous absurdity is the only way to counter malignant absurdity. And thankfully, often enough there are events in nature and human affairs that are so delightful and beautiful that funny tributes must be drawn.

There are strange times, however, when a cartoonist just wants to declare: Look, I am not wise enough to understand this complex predicament called human existence, this injury called life; today I have no meaningful comment to make to newspaper readers. All I want to do is confess my helpless naivety in front of this overpowering culture of cynical cleverness, confess it in the form of a mystical or primal drawing from the heart, because on some days, in a world poisoned by rabid commentary, that's the most useful and valuable thing an artist can offer. It's what an artist can do and *must* do – and besides, if I don't do it, who else will? I'd better do it.

And so here it is.

MORNING COFFEE WITH WOES OF THE WORLD AND DUCK   Leunig

When your world is feeling stuck
Climb upon a big white duck
Sail away across the dark.
Out towards the little spark

When you reach that tiny star
Put it safely in a jar
Say a prayer and give a quack,
Take it out and put it back;

Put it back and let it be,
Sparkling above the sea,
Above the sea so dark and deep
As you quack yourself to sleep.

Leunig

Help me doctor I'm having these episodes of compassion.
A little bit won't hurt...
No, this is serious; it's full blown; it's spilling out all over the place
You mean it's... it's... INDISCRIMINATE COMPASSION?
YES! I'm feeling sympathy and sadness for humans regardless of their race, religion, nationality or politics...
Oh dear... Have you tried xenophobia the old traditional remedy...?
It doesn't work.... I just have to face the fact that I feel sorry for everyone..
You may have been abused as a child.... too much love and understanding perhaps.
Leunig

IT'S NOT EASY TO KEEP YOUR CHIN UP IN THESE DARK AND DIFFICULT TIMES.

NORMAL
CHIN
POSITION

CHIN STARTS
TO GO UP BUT
MOUTH STARTS
TO GO DOWN
IN RESPONSE.

CHIN FULLY UP BUT
MOUTH TOTALLY DOWN.
POSTURE RIDICULOUS.
A BAD LOOK CONVEYING
A SENSE OF STUPIDITY,
MISERY AND DESPAIR.

Leunig

POLITICIAN WITH CONSCIENCE AND PERSONAL ADVISER

My dear friends, I may
have lost some vital parts of
my mental health and I want
you to help me find them.

Leunig

YOU CAN RELY ON IT; THIS little group — this HOUSEHOLD is 100% SANE.
The woman is 40% SANE
The man is 30% SANE
The hound is 30% SANE....
.... making a collective, working sanity of exactly 100% (OPTIMUM)
If one of the group has an "episode", causing, for example, a 10% loss of sanity, the remaining two will set about making up the shortfall.
By a supreme effort of will, discipline and concentration the remaining two will each generate an extra 5% sanity. The problem is that the effort involved may cause the eyes to bulge in such a manner that the entire situation looks TOTALLY MAD.
Leunig

SOLEMNISATION

We are gathered here together to consolidate this person into a state of complete singleness.

If anybody has any problem with that, let's hear about it now or forever remain quiet.

Do you take yourself to be utterly single, to the exclusion of all others forever?

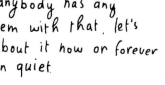

I DO.

WITH THIS RING I SINGLE MYSELF AND ALL MY WORLDLY GOODS ARE MINE AND NOBODY ELSE'S

I now pronounce you completely and utterly single.

① THE SINGLE HAS THE RIGHT TO KISS HERSELF OR HIMSELF AND TO SELF SPRINKLE WITH CONFETTI.

② THE SINGLE HAS THE RIGHT TO THROW THE BOUQUET INTO THE CROWD

③ THE SINGLE HAS THE RIGHT TO A RECEPTION AND A HONEYMOON

④ SOMETIMES HONEYMOONS ARE A DISASTER PARTICULARLY WHEN SINGLES MEET OTHER SINGLES AND FALL IN LOVE; IN WHICH CASE THE SINGLENESS DOES NOT WORK AND MUST BE ANNULLED.

BLUSH — BLUSH

Leunig

FIND LOVE TODAY — MEET COMPATIBLE SINGLES NEAR YOU.

A SINGLE small wispy cloud
floating across the sky.
You may have a lot in common.

A single dog standing smiling
on the footpath; seemingly at peace
but obviously not knowing what's
happening, and not caring.
You may get along very well.

A single tabby cat sitting hunched
in the back lane, looking worried
and wary.
You may understand each other.

A single old snail of considerable
experience making slow but steady
progress up the side of a rubbish bin
Perhaps a soul mate.

Leunig

They were made for each other.
It was a match made in heaven.
It was meant to be.

They were inseparable.
They went everywhere
together.

He was mesmerised. He was devoted.
He only had eyes for his beloved.

Until at last: WEDDING BELLS!
....I now pronounce
you man and phone.
You may kiss the device.

Leunig

HOW TO KNOW IF YOUR PANTS ARE ON FIRE

Get the new PANTS ON FIRE app for your phone.

Receive ALERTS when the seat of your trousers goes up in flames.

GET UPDATES on progress of fire and reports on how your bottom is faring in the blaze.

BE THE FIRST TO KNOW.
BUY
PANTS ON FIRE APP
NOW

Leunig

Modern Stupid

It's much easier to go stupid these days than in previous times

Now we can do it faster and with more comfort and convenience thanks to modern methods and technology.

Back in the old days they had to do it all by hand. It was sheer drudgery

You can easily fit it into a busy life. It's available to everybody; right there at your fingertips.

leunig

Get off my selfie stick
you egotistical narcissist.

Leunig

Those people — who are they?
What's it like to be somebody else? Look at them — they're everywhere! The others!
Those OTHER people. Those people who are not you.
What do they want? Why do they exist? Look at them! Lots and lots of them but each one alone.
Those people who are somebody else. They seem so weird and strange. What do they get up to?
What do you do with people who are not you? What do you do with yourself? What do you get up to? How come?
Leunig

INTERVIEW WITH AN AUTUMN LEAF

Q.   How would you describe yourself?

A.L.   Dead, I suppose. Finished.

Q.   How did this happen?

A.L.   I just couldn't hold on any longer.
I let go and down I fluttered. It felt OK.
My work was done. I'd had enough.

Q.   You mean you couldn't take it any more?

A.L.   No. I mean I was satisfied. I'd had a
good enough life. I guess I was happy.

Q.   What were the high points?

A.L.   I can't remember. It was all pretty good.

Q.   Any advice to the readers?

A.L.   No. Not really.

Q.   Thank you.

A.L.   My pleasure.

Leunig

In a faraway paddock, the Opposite of racing: The Spring Carnival of Quiet Stillness.

Where do dorks go
during fashion week?

Dorks can quickly
scramble into these pipes
if they see a fashion
person approaching.

They hide in concrete pipes
which are placed on the streets
as temporary fashion shelters
by the city council.

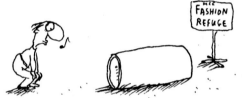

They lie in the pipes and eat
sardine sandwiches and
chicken noodle soup until it is
safe to come out.

Leunig

THE ORIGIN AND MEANING OF TENNIS

Tennis was invented in Ely, Cambridgeshire, England in 1632 by Lord Tennis.

He wondered if his sadness might leave him if he were to throw the ball away. So he threw it over the front fence.

Lord Tennis suffered from melancholia and felt his sadness to be round in shape and located in his chest.

The ball landed in the street in front of a passing minstrel who took a swipe at it with his lute and the ball hurtled back to the amazed Lord.

The eccentric Lord created a small leather ball to symbolically represent this sadness so that he could contemplate it more effectively.

In great excitement the Lord took his own lute and belted the ball back into the street and the first "Tennis match" then took place with the "ball of melancholia". The deep symbolism of tennis still lives on to this very day.

Leunig

PRESS CONFERENCE

The Sheffield Shield will now be called "The Pura Milk Cup."

Christmas will henceforth be called King Calypso Cordials.

New year's eve will be known as Pressure Ace Hydraulic Hoses.

 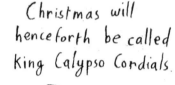  

And the season of summer will be renamed, Big Horizon Asphalt Supplies. Are there any questions?

Mr. Richards; do you think the world is going mad more rapidly than usual...?

Before I answer, I'd like to correct you; my name is not Richards; it's Crinkle Valley Hot Kettle Country Potato Chips. What was the question again?

It's O.K.

Leunig

DINKUM AUSSIE AUSTRALIA DAY DIARY

8 A.M.
WOKE UP WITH AN
AUSSIE FLAG IN MY
BED AND MADE LOVE
TO IT. WHAT A
BEAUTIFUL EXPERIENCE

11 AM.
SAT ON THE COUCH WITH
ANOTHER AUSSIE FLAG,
COMMUNICATING TOGETHER
IN SILENCE.   AWESOME

9 A.M
GOT UP AND ATE TWO
AUSSIE FLAGS FOR
BREAKFAST.
BEAUTIFUL !

1 PM
LUNCH. ATE ANOTHER
THREE AUSSIE FLAGS.
BIG ONES.
I LOVE THAT FLAG!

10 AM.
RAISED AUSSIE FLAG
ON FLAGPOLE AND
WEPT UNCONTROLLABLY.

I'M IN LOVE.

2.30 PM
AFTERNOON NAP.
I DREAMED I WAS
AN AUSSIE FLAG AND
I MET THIS OTHER AUSSIE
FLAG AND WE FELL IN LOVE
AND DID AMAZING THINGS.
WHAT A HORNY DREAM.
WHAT A GREAT DAY.

Leunig

THE SIGNIFICANCE OF WOMEN'S HANDBAGS

There is much to be considered regarding the meaning and symbolism of women's handbags.

But perhaps handbags represent another existence: a life dreamed of but not achieved in reality:

Some say that a handbag speaks volumes about a woman's love-life and associated "issues".

...a well-made, beautiful life with secure buckles, zippers and many snug compartments to fill with amazing things: A life you can get a handle on.

And indeed, hours of fun and pleasure can be had observing and interpreting handbags with this theory in mind.

Another theory: the more exotic and dazzling a woman's handbag — the more boring her partner. Too many handbags means trouble.

Leunig

A FAIRLY TYPICAL DISCUSSION
What profit a man if he gain the whole world but lose his soul.....?
Well, we've done a few figures on that and you might be pleasantly surprised because it seems that there is QUITE a profit Quite a NICE profit in fact...
and what would the profit be like if you lost, say, half your soul and gained only half the world?
Still very nice! It's a huge audience — a huge market and I'd like you to consider the following: I know a man who has only one sixteenth of his soul left and he's perfectly happy — perfectly happy!!
Leunig

Twinkle, twinkle little star
What a boring thing you are
When compared with fireworks
Stars are lonely, loser jerks.
Twinkle twinkle little star
How embarrassing you are.

leunig

Summer Diary

Yesterday, normality was supposed to return but it didn't.

"There was no such thing as normality" said a smart looking fellow "it was all a bloody lie" He was so sure of himself.

"...it's not coming back," said a man in the street, "...It's all finished; kaput!"

I believed in it, although I couldn't really prove it existed — nor could I describe it very well..

"They've stopped making it," said the lady in the shop, "...discontinued! people weren't using it, too slow!"

...except to say that it seemed to hold everything together more or less.
Anyway I'm going to miss normality for the time being but I'm not giving up hope. I need it.

Leunig

BRAINSTORM '08 CANBERRA
We thank you for your presentation Professor McLintock, but you haven't explained how the nation is going to benefit from these solar-powered bagpipes...
Leunig

Moments of no consequence
Seem to make a lot of sense;
Like the gentle pitter patter
Of the things that do not matter
As I sit alone and stare;
Neither here and neither there.

Leunig

This day before you now
Greet her with love and joy.
She is a fine strong person:
This precious living day
She is young and old
She is warm and cold
She is here for you
She will hold you well.
Make love with her
You'd be a fool to turn away
She is here. She is yours.
She is wise, she is hers.
She has dawned on you; this epic day.
Do not underestimate what she can do
Give thanks for her as you make your way.
Give thanks for the power and the kindness
Of this precious living day

Leunig

Give the all-clear signal. It's not a shark, it's a big piece of human faeces with a dorsal fin.
Leunig

The SAUSAGE TAX has risen to <u>25%</u>

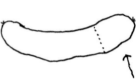

Further more... Loose change in pockets will be subject to a tax of 20%

One quarter of every sausage must now be set aside and sent to the treasurer.

Coins found underneath couch cushions or on the floor in bedrooms will be taxed at a whopping $33\frac{1}{3}\%$

Alternatively - one in every four sausages can be sent but must include a squeeze of tomato sauce.

Revenue raised will be used to maintain and protect the government sausage stockpile — so crucial in the war against <u>terror</u>.

Leunig

I went into the man cave
To ease my male sadness
And in this awful enclave
I pondered on my badness.

"You bad-bad, bad-bad person"
An angry voice berated.
My shame began to worsen
And I disintegrated.

I staggered to the duck pen
Quacking and despairing
And so I came unstuck then
All happy and uncaring.

On the pillow, in the Spring
Appears a strange and magic thing
A bright surprise, all damp and cool:
The afternoon saliva pool.

A little kip, a weary nap.
A pixie turns the secret tap
And out it drips, the happy drool:
The afternoon saliva pool.

Such truth and poetry it speaks
As from the peaceful mouth it leaks;
Scripture from the holy fool:
The afternoon saliva pool.

Leunig

BUILT BY AUSTRALIANS IN ALTONA

1.

2.

THE HYBRID CAR THAT WILL SAVE THE WORLD

3.

The amazing hybrid car is made by crossing
a 1954 model three wheeled car (fig. 1) with a
Louis XV porcelain mantel clock (fig. 2) which
produces a one wheeled, three legged Louis XV
marquetry bureau of exquisite proportions and
refinement (fig. 3). When released onto the market
it is expected to save the planet from doom.

Leunig

NATIONAL INFRASTRUCTURE

THE DULL CUBE PROJECT.
A giant concrete cube for every town, city and suburb in the land.

THE ARCH OF NOTHING.
GATEWAY TYPE ARCHES ON A GRAND SCALE TO BE CONSTRUCTED IN CIVIC SPACES ACROSS THE NATION

THE ARCH OF NOTHING

THE NATIONAL TOOTHPASTE GRID.
A PIPELINE LOOPING AROUND THE CONTINENT TO DELIVER TOOTHPASTE TO EVERY BATHROOM IN AUSTRALIA.

THE SOLAR SAUSAGE SIZZLER PROJECT.
SAUSAGE SIZZLE PANELS TO BE INSTALLED ON EVERY ROOFTOP IN THE LAND

Leunig

EVERYBODY IS TIRED

Everywhere you go...
Everybody is tired.

So exhausted that
she has gone into
a strange euphoric
trance and is
hallucinating.

I'm not tired

Except for one peculiar
woman who claims she
is not tired.

So just recapping...
EVERYBODY IS
TIRED.

Upon closer investigation
however, it is discovered
that she is utterly
EXHAUSTED

Except for this one
poor, wretched and
deluded woman who
is deeply radically
EXHAUSTED.

Leunig

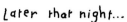

Hurtful people go away
I am going out to play
With my pixie hat and bell
With the goat I love so well
With the duck of wistful prayer
With its wise and lovely stare.
With our friend the honey bee.
We will make our monastery.

Leunig

An emissions trading scheme simply means that if I refrain from releasing a polluting emission then I get a credit...
sure, and not only will I give you full credit mate, I'll also be eternally grateful...
Leunig

FRUIT DRIVEN.
THE NOSE IS PILLOWS,
SHEETS, BLANKETS.
IN THE MOUTH IT IS
SOFT AND WARM WITH
GOOD SUPPORT. A
NICELY SPRUNG WINE
WITH A SLOW FINISH

SLEEPY CREEK PINOT NOIR

EMPTY PADDOCK CHARDONNAY

FRUIT DRIVEN.

BREEZY AROMAS OF
DRY GRASS, GRANITE BOULDERS,
FENCE POSTS, MUSHROOMS and
THISTLES.
THE PALATE IS BROAD,
UNDULATING WITH SOME
LIGHT CLOUDS AT THE
FINISH — WITH A LONE
COW AND A RABBIT.

BLACK HOLE ESTATE LATE PICKED SHIRAZ

FRUIT DRIVEN.

WILD BUSTLING VAPOURS
OF ROTTING KAPOK, OLD
BOOKS, MELTED LIPSTICK,
BURNT TOAST AND CAR
UPHOLSTERY. IN THE
MOUTH THERE IS THE SOFT
SLIPPERY SENSATION OF A
TONGUE WHICH IS POINTY
AT THE FINISH.

WINE WRITER'S TUNNEL CLASSIC NOUVEAU '99

FRUIT DRIVEN
FRUIT DRIVEN
FRUIT DRIVEN
BANANAS, COCONUTS, PAW PAWS
PINEAPPLES, CHOCOLATE, MINT
TOFFEE, TOBACCO, KIT-KAT
MARS BARS, COFFEE,
PARKING FINES, LOVE
LETTERS...AND... UMM...

FRUIT DRIVEN!

Leunig

After decades of faithful service to the nation, a man retires from politics.

Joe Bloggs: humble constituent, careful voter and informed citizen has decided to chuck in the towel.

He believed in the political process, he followed the issues and debates, he dreamed of an intelligent world.

EXIT

A PARTING WORD FROM JOE:

What a fool I was...

Leunig

It's Summer, and nature has made some special arrangements for you.

At the start of each day during summer you will be allotted your own personal fly.

This common house fly will attend to you tirelessly throughout the day wherever you go.

You will get to know each other well as the day proceeds and as the temperature rises.

Sometimes a group of flies will be provided and they will work as a team with you.

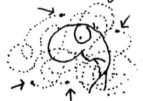

All day long they will be dedicated, skilful, energetic and totally enthusiastic.

At the end of the day, they will depart, and next morning a fresh new team will arrive to continue with Mother Nature's amazing project.

Leunig

MODERN CREATURE: PART-TIME, PART-MAN, PART-GHOST.

PART-TIME WORK

PART-TIME RECREATION

PART-TIME RELATIONSHIP

PART-TIME REST

Leunig

I want to be a Lycra man and have a Lycra life
With Lycra covered children and a Lycra covered wife;
A rooster clad in Lycra that will wake me in the dawn
A dog with Lycra underpants he wears while watching porn.
A handkerchief, a table cloth, a pillowslip, a flag;
A Lycra life and then at last... a Lycra body bag.

Leunig

A KISS

He never thought she'd be a frump
She never thought he'd be a grump
They never thought their circumstance
would be as strange as this...
She hung her head and had a weep
He went to bed but couldn't sleep
They couldn't understand it
So they settled for a kiss.

Leunig

Life is _Offensive_ and refuses to apologise.

The rose bush — an arch conservative with cruel thorns.

DEATH — the right-wing radical.

The heartless, dull bureaucracy of time.

The cat? The cat is probably a monarchist!

The dog — a naked opportunist; a moral vacuum; an uneducated, pleasure-driven philistine.

And the moon — so aloof, so cold so full of itself.

Leunig

THE SAD STORY OF VICTIM HOOD.

My mum's name was Victoria
My father's name was Tim.
Half my name I got from her
The other half from him
My mother wasn't very bright
My dad was really dumb
So VICTIM was the name I got
Which made me rather glum
"VICTIM, VICTIM, VICTIM"
It never sounded good
And furthermore I'm sad to say
My second name was HOOD.

Leunig

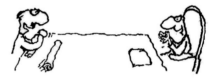

Leunig

Oh violent bogan drunk and dumb
You got sprayed with capsicum
For brawling in the streets at night
It's little wonder that you fight,
Considering the way we are;
The fury of the motor car
The violence of every sort
From film to politics and sport,
The secret fears we can't discuss;
Men and women, them and us,
The way our culture has been made.
Perhaps it's time we all got sprayed.

Leunig

The Public toiler wall
Where people used to Scrawl
Their Naughty SMUT
HAS turned INto a glut
Of something SEEDIER...
Social MediA !

Leunig

Leunig

THE SOUND OF DEMOCRACY

The sound of democracy is the sound of constant bickering.

Besmirching. Denouncing. Attacking.

It's a lovely sound and a wonderful influence on the human heart.

The details are forgotten and what remains is the spirit of tribal aggression, pomposity and mean stupidity.

The policies are not so important; what matters is the enduring tone.

It is the tone that will rule the country.

Leunig

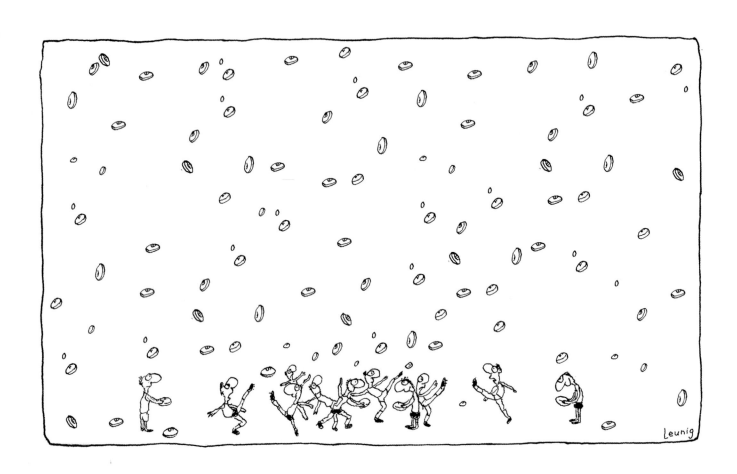

PRAYER AND CONFESSION

I am a football refugee
I had to pack my bag
and flee
From all the kicking and
concussion
The endless vacuous
discussion
Of grunting men with
balls and boots
I really couldn't give
two hoots
For all this domineering
guff;
The howling mob, the
rough and tough,
The taking up of
so much space,
The shameless shoving
in our face.
The tribal nonsense
soaked in beer.
God please get me
out of here.

Leunig

One of the most AMAZING and SIGNIFICANT events of the twentieth Century took Place on a creaking bed in a small hut on a remote WINDSWEPT HILLSIDE in rural Australia many years ago....

To this day nobody has ever revealed what happened!

Leunig

Family Drinking Patterns

Daughter Emily is a <u>BINGE</u> drinker: she drinks alcohol at parties.

Mother is a <u>CRINGE</u> drinker: she pretends she doesn't like alcohol, but she really likes it a lot.

Father is a <u>WHINGE</u> drinker: He drinks alcohol and starts grizzling and being grouchy.

Son Jack is a <u>SPONGE</u> drinker: he soaks it up effortlessly in vast, amazing quantities.

Daughter Melissa is a <u>LUNGE</u> drinker: she grabs it desperately wherever she can.

Son James is a <u>GRUNGE</u> drinker: he drinks cheap wine at band practice or in the park.

Leunig

you are charged with failing to attend a new year's eve celebration. How do you plead?
I was suffering from a bout of NONCHALANCE your honour.. I plead temporary insanity
NONCHALANCE! NONCHALANCE!!? After all the media has offered you? All the build-up, the television specials, the newspaper lift-outs, the reviews of the 20th century... the hundreds and hundreds of LISTS of best things... the thousands of columnists and commentators...
...all pouring their hearts out about the new millennium - telling you their inner most personal secret wisdoms and anecdotes - just so that you can be..... NONCHALANT!??
I'm ordering you into counselling... and I'm going to SHAME you... You can wear a sign in public for six months.
S. BLOGGS NONCHALANCE COUNSELLOR D.NC. M.
I MISSED OUT ON A MAJOR EVENT
Leunig

Darling, it's hell out there.
It's so good to come home
to the simple things:
an alcohol binge,
a gluttonous rampage
and a wild sex orgy...

Leunig

HOW TO REMAIN CALM

The world has got the economic jitters.

It's time to stop jittering with the world. It's time to find your own personal jitter and jitter in your own unique little way.

You can feel it; shaking, rattling, vibrating.

As the world jitters to its beat, you can jitter to the off-beat... Jitter and counter-jitter.

Things are wobbly. Things are jittery.

Oh dear... what to do?

These two opposing jitters offset each other's energy and momentum, and the shake is neutralised.

THUS YOU ACHIEVE CALM

Leunig

HELL

Hell has a very large mechanical roof which can be closed to block out the good weather.

Hell has a vast, open, central area of lush, green grass and you're not allowed on it.

Hell has plastic seats from which you may look at the forbidden grassy area — or you may choose to look at it while standing on concrete or steel. You have a choice.

Hell has restaurants, bars, nightclubs, retail outlets, cafés, underground car parks and many corporate boxes...

— all with television screens showing the untouchable green green grass.

The tiers of hell can also be moved mechanically and can handle huge volumes of people quietly and efficiently. The road to Hell is paved with good inventions.

leunig

THE INCREDIBLE EXCITEMENT OF LEADERSHIP ASPIRATION

Leunig

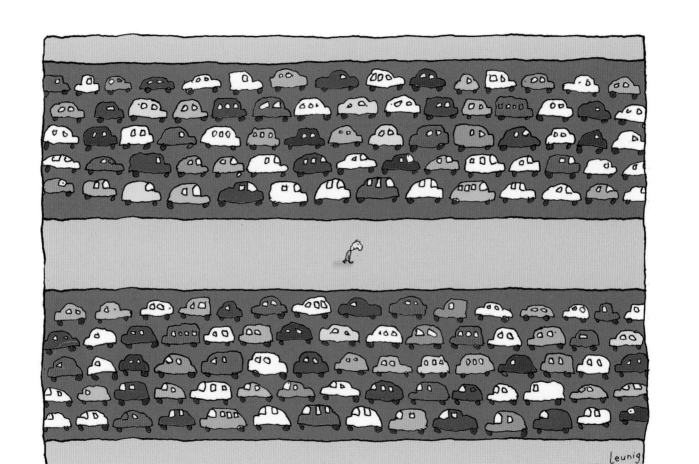

LAMENT WITH YEARNING.

GOOD GOVERNMENT AND
A VOTE FOR EVERY CITIZEN;
THESE THINGS ARE FINE...

YET WHAT USE ARE THEY
WITHOUT A BIRD SINGING
UPON EVERY HEAD?

FOR EVERY SOUL —
BIRD MUSIC,
BIRD HAPPINESS,
BIRD FEELING.

BUT OUR BIRDS LEAVE —
AND SADNESS BEGINS
TO ARRIVE.

WHY DO THE BIRDS
LEAVE US? DO OUR
HEADS BECOME TOO LOUD
AND HARSH AND BUSY?

COME BACK LITTLE
BIRD, MY HEAD IS
SAFE NOW. IT IS CALM
WITH SADNESS.
I AM READY.

Leunig

Amid the great cacophony
Of angry words and commentary,
A sudden bright epiphany.

It was small and soft and clear,
It was far and it was near.
A little bird was in my ear.

And all the endless arguments
The fierce aggression and defence
Quite suddenly made little sense.

Instead the secret of the bird,
So vast and deep and true was heard.
It only sang one simple word.

Another Little Mystery

He used to talk to himself but not any more; now he whispered to himself — and quite frequently too.

'PSST--SSP
MMM--SS-RR-SES
MABDRPST--SISS..

One day he stopped in his tracks:
"SPEAK UP OR SHUT UP AND forever hold your peace!", he cried to himself in desperation.

Wherever he went the whispering went with him — the trouble was, he couldn't quite hear what he was whispering; it was so soft.

After that the whispering stopped and never returned. He became stricken with a forlorn sense that a huge and vital revelation had been lost to him forever.

Soft, yet it sounded very much in earnest — as if it were an important secret or a dire warning — but he just couldn't quite hear what it was.

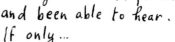

If only he'd gone somewhere still and quiet and slow and had just listened patiently and been able to hear.
If only...

Leunig

ORGANS AND GLANDS

The pineal gland is tiny
And when the sun is shiny
It gathers in the light
And makes us feel all right

The mind is quite mysterious
It's funny and it's serious
It searches for delight
And makes us feel all right

The heart has got its ways
To make a little blaze
That burns all through the night
And makes us feel all right.

Leunig

ANNOUNCEMENT.

A very limited period of time is coming when no festival, celebration or major event will be making a claim upon your existence

And there will be no logo, no poster, no slogan. There will be the dripping of the tap, the ticking of the clock and the coming and going of plain and ordinary things.

Perhaps it could be called "ordinary time" or "peace" or "ordinary life". It has no official name. It may not last very long

Perhaps you will also hear a bird sing or a spoon move in a bowl or a person whistling over the back fence or the sound of pruning secateurs on a rose bush. Who knows.

There will be no fireworks. nor will there be a release of doves or balloons; nor will there be "special offers" of any kind and no "information hot line"

There will be no media coverage; no commentary or analysis. It will all pass unremarked upon. Are you ready?

Leunig

LAMENT

As I lay sleeping
The graffiti boy came creeping;
Creeping through the dark
To make a boring mark
That made no sense
Upon the paling fence.

I can recall
When old Jack Frost would call
As I lay curled;
He painted half the world
In sparkling white;
And always got it right.

Leunig

AMERICAN MILITARY OPERATIONS IN IRAQ

OPERATION
IRAQI FREEDOM

OPERATION DESERT SCORPION
OPERATION IRON BULLET

OPERATION EAGLE CURTAIN
OPERATION BAYONET LIGHTNING
OPERATION PANTHER SQUEEZE

OPERATION CHOKE HOLD
OPERATION IRON HAMMER

OPERATION DEVIL SIPHON
OPERATION IRON JUSTICE

SIR, WE'VE RUN
OUT OF RIDICULOUS
MACHO CODE NAMES...

O.K.
JOB'S DONE.
LET'S GET
OUT OF HERE.

Leunig

WISDOM FOR THE DAY

"GENTLEMEN MAKE PASSES AT WOMEN WHO WEAR NATIVE GRASSES."

Leunig

THE WAY.

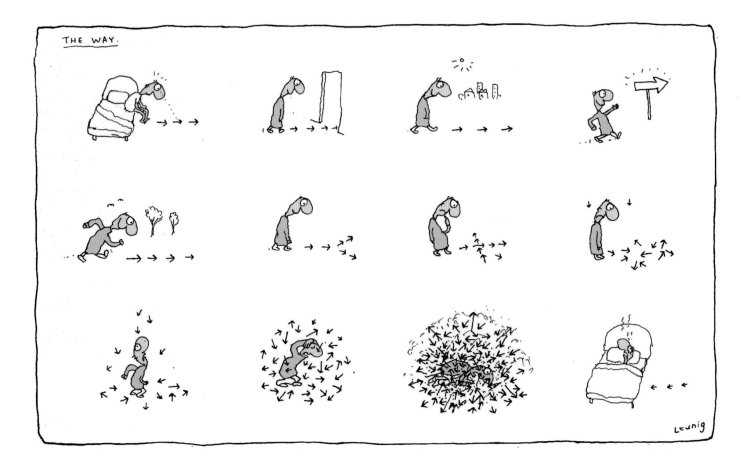

Leunig

RECENT ONE-PERSON CONVOYS PAST THE FRONT WINDOW

The convoy of
no confidence

The convoy of
total amazement

The convoy of
sweet nonchalance

The convoy of
utter bewilderment

The convoy of
amused disbelief

The convoy of
oh well, ho hum.

Leunig

OUR AMAZING DOG

SIT   ROLL OVER

NOW...
BE AT PEACE.
BE KIND.
FORGIVE.

LOVE...
REFLECT UPON
LIFE'S GREAT
BEAUTY AND
SADNESS.

Leunig

MOTHERS DAY GIFT IDEAS FOR THOSE WHO HAVE A DIFFICULT AND PAINFUL RELATIONSHIP WITH THEIR MOTHER

A prayer to a candle and a flower.

A few coins to a weary beggar

A song to grandmother moon

Some bread for the birds.

Leunig

PRAYER FOR FATHERS DAY

Our Father
Who art uneven;
Mellowed be thy name,
Thy kingdom come and gone,
Thy will has been a bit worn down
Here on earth, so far from heaven.
Give us this day our daily joke
And forgive yourself for telling it
As we forgive you for telling it.
And lead us, not particularly,
But deliver us your dear self
For thine is the thingdom,
The flower and the story
Forever and ever,
Ah men.

Leunig

APPS FOR TROUBLED TIMES   HELPING YOU THROUGH THE CRISIS

QUACK PRO DUCK TRANSLATOR

Ever wondered what your ducks are talking about? Find out with Quack Pro Duck Translator.

TEA BREAK

Click on this app and your device shuts down for fifteen minutes and will not restart.

BEDTIME DELUXE

Sick of clever commentary going nowhere? Of course you are. Listen to four old reliable bedtime stories and go to sleep: Little Red Riding Hood, Jack and the Bean Stalk, Goldilocks and the Three Bears, The Tortoise and the Hare.

PINKY-PURPLES

Gaze in silence at a host of pleasant pinkish purple shades and be well pleased.

PORRIDGE MUSIC

Fifty rousing tunes to go with your morning porridge featuring the Big Breakfast Brass Band.

EARTHWORM

One hundred famous poems in praise of our friend, the humble earthworm.

Leunig

MAKE YOUR OWN LEGAL PERFORMANCE ENHANCING ORGANIC FOOTY SUPPLEMENT
OLD SECRET BUSH RECIPE - AMAZING RESULTS.

INGREDIENTS:

Ten used leather footy boots. CIRCA: 1950's One bottle of tomato sauce. One bucket of water. One pint of urine from the milkman's horse.

Place bucket in the woodshed and allow to ferment for THREE WEEKS. Strain mixture, bottle liquid and store in cool place.

METHOD:

Chop boots into tiny pieces and boil in water. When mixture is cool, add sauce and urine into the bucket and stir.

Take a warm bath on the night before match. Add one cup of mixture to bath water. Drink another cup of mixture next day immediately before match. Good luck.

Leunig

If life is a
meat pie....

A little dab?
A big squirt?

...and sport is
tomato sauce...

One whole bottle?
Two bottles?
Twenty-seven bottles?

...then how much of
this tomato sauce do we
place upon our pie?

Perhaps it depends upon
how awful or how delicious
the pie is — or how
good the sauce is .or
how mad you are.

Leunig

THE MILITARISATION OF EVERYDAY LIFE.

OPERATION CLEAN SWEEP

OPERATION BLACK FANG

OPERATION IRON RESOLVE

OPERATION GOLDEN SURGE

OPERATION HELLFIRE

OPERATION DARK HOLE

Leunig

THE ELITE SPECIAL FORCES OF AUTUMN

The Yellow Devils

QUINCE LOGISTICS TASK FORCE.
JAM AND PASTE.

The Green Beanies

TOMATO CHUTNEY SPECIAL OPERATIONS
RAPID RESPONSE GROUP.

The Black Forks.

COMPOST COMMANDOS.
BOOTS ON THE GROUND.

The Fungal Rangers

RECONNAISSANCE STRIKE TEAM
TAKING out mushrooms with
Speed and deadly accuracy.

Leunig

Late last night when all was dark
I thought I heard a moron bark
And as the sound began to die
I heard another one reply

My blood ran cold, my skin turned grey
Remembering election day
Was not so terribly remote
And morons had the right to vote!

And then the sound became a din
As more and more morons joined in
And suddenly I realised
That they were getting organised

Australia has some nasty things
The crocodile, the fish that stings,
The snake, the spider and the shark
But worst of all, the moron's bark!

Leunig

Into weariness and woe
I am bound to simply go,
Understanding less and less
Of this existential mess.
Not to stagger or to stoop
But to bear this bowl of soup
With careful steadiness and cheer;
This soup I made, this bowl so dear,
This time on earth, these bits I found,
The trembling heart, the shaky ground,
The fading light, the wistful moon,
My winding path, my wooden spoon.

So I went into the garden and set out to dig my air raid shelter for the forthcoming war.

Before long, I was eating potatoes for lunch — garnished with rosemary, olive oil, lemon juice — and sprinkled with salt and pepper.

Soon I came upon some potatoes, and they looked pretty good.

Thoroughly delicious! Then I lay down for an afternoon nap and had a wonderful dream...so peaceful and beautiful...

I gathered them up, took them inside, washed them and put them on the stove to boil.

I woke up happy and refreshed. Now where was I? Ah yes; the air raid shelter for the forthcoming nuclear war. Back to work!

Leunig

Mail to be relied upon,
Not tampered with or spied upon
May be written on a paper smidgen
And carried by a trusty pigeon.

P-Mail is the safest way
To send the words you want to say
Winging out across the blue:
"Mother Nature, I love you."

Mr Curly's going mad
Things that make the people glad
Only seem to make him sad
Mr. Curly's lonely

Something awful's in the air
Yet nobody seems to care
Cup of tea, the only prayer.
Mr. Curly's lonely.

Leunig

Dear Mr. Curly...
  I must tell you that I am having trouble being alert and alarmed — or fearful about the so-called "forces of evil". As a wise woman once said, "Nothing in life is to be feared, it is only to be understood". Fine words, but the truth is that I don't fear OR understand... and what's more, I don't really care. I am a complete and utter failure at all this hateful dread. It seems to me that I have no time or energy for listening to warnings from powerful, important people who seem to me very untrustworthy and ridiculous. Perhaps I am too fascinated and engaged with my direction-finding duck, which provides me with such a warm abundance of wisdom, joy and companionship... and therefore much protection and security.

Am I being delusional or foolish? If I am, then I highly recommend it as a real source of contentment and good humour, even in these sad and serious times. Do you have a view on this matter?
  With love...
  and peaceful dabbling sounds.
  Vasco Pyjama.

Leunig

Mr. Curly spies on himself.

He sits quietly beneath a tree and gives a sigh.

A sigh is the password. His defences drop. He goes inside.

Carefully, slowly he enters the inner sanctum.

And there the secrets: 'KNOW THYSELF' and 'MIND YOUR OWN BUSINESS'

Leunig

I miss those old Australian blokes
Who had a way of making jokes;
They spoke in fluent Curly;
A language I learned early.

In truth it was my native tongue;
Not spoken hard and fast, but sung
Or whistled, hummed and sighed
Or simply felt inside.

In these times of gaffes and slurs
And deep offence when someone errs
In all the hurly-burly;
Oh how I long for Curly.

Lone Voyager Vasco Pyjama delivers the keynote address at the annual conference for pixies, ducks and brown butterflies in Curly Flat.

The Curly-Pyjama Letters

Dear Mr. Curly,

wandering alone in the world as I am, I notice that food prices are rising at an alarming rate. In my quest for good value and frugal living I have discovered in my local grocery shop that a small packet of bicarb-soda can be purchased for the remankably low price of one dollar and sixty-nine cents, and a small packet of linseed can be bought for a mere one dollar and forty-nine cents. These discoveries have cheered me up immensely and I feel compelled to share this good news with the world, particulary with those who are struggling on limited budgets. The question is: do you know any recipes for dishes made only of linseeds and bicarbonate of soda? In these troubled times I eagerly await your reply.

Yours Sincerely
Vasco Pyjama.

GROCERY SHOP

FRESH VEGIE PIES

Leunig

Mr. Curly Blesses the Fleet.

As belligerence in the world increases and military escalation grows, Mr. Curly reviews the Curly Flat navy by the shores of Lake Lacuna and blesses the fleet. He then announces a massive boost to the flotilla, of three fine healthy young ducks; an announcement which is met by much joyous quacking and splashing about.

Leunig

THE CURLY-PYJAMA LETTERS

Dear Vasco,
...just a letter to remind you that the Festival of Not Too Much will soon be happening in Curly Flat. Naturally there are no great expectations and it all happens without too much fuss; nothing costs too much, not too many people are involved, nothing is too noisy and there is nothing too amazing happening. IT'S REALLY LOVELY, and no fireworks... HOORAY. Perhaps we will meet and take part in the curly duck dance for some free-form pleasure and fun. Actually it's not really a festival — it's a get-together. The word 'FESTIVAL' seems a bit too much. Anyway, hoping to see you before too long.

  Yours truly Mr. Curly.

Leunig

CURLY PYJAMA

Mr. Curly, Vasco Pyjama and the direction-finding duck enjoy a concert by the Curly Flat Bird Choir. Never has Handel's Hallelujah Chorus sounded so joyous. Never has gratitude about life been felt so deeply. Never before have the woes of the world seemed so bearable. And never has the duck been heard to quack so eagerly. Indeed a good omen for the summer and the year to come.

leunig

§ Poem from Vasco Pyjama to Mr. Curly.

My dearest Mister Curly
Today I woke up early
And made a little wish:
That we were flying fish,
Sparkling and free.
We jumped out of the sea
And flew up to the sun.
Then after that was done,
We went down to explore
The deepest ocean floor.
And so we did discover
The most amazing lover,
For what it may be worth,
It really is the earth.

Leunig